Especially for

_____

From

_____

Date

_____

© 2011 by Barbour Publishing, Inc.

Compiled and written by Nicole O'Dell.

ISBN 978-1-61626-196-2

Published by Barbour Publishing, Inc., P.O. Box 719, Uhrichsville, Ohio 44683, www.barbourbooks.com

Our mission is to publish and distribute inspirational products offering exceptional value and biblical encouragement to the masses.

Printed in China.

Girl Talk

Nicole O'Dell

BARBOUR
PUBLISHING

BFF

Best Friends Forever.
Lasting friendships—the "forever" part—are rare.
Be the friend you want to have. Loyal.
Trustworthy. Generous.

The Mirror

What stares back at you when you gaze into the mirror?
You're changing so fast, you might not even recognize
the person you see. Ask Jesus to show you the beauty
He sees in that reflection. You are perfect to Him.

Love the Unlovable

You know those kids who get picked on?
The ones who are different for some reason?
Jesus would befriend them before He would the popular
kids. You can be an extension of His love by reaching
out to people others just push away.

Mentor

A mentor is someone who helps *you* do what *she's* already
mastered. Who, in your life, has already become the woman
you want to someday be? Find her, plant yourself beside her,
watch what she does, then do it.

Somebody Said

"Somebody told somebody else what she heard somebody say."
Then it must be true, right? Gossip spread like that can do so
much harm to other people, and it's often nowhere near the truth.
Be a spreader of truth and love, not mistrust and lies.

Ready, Set, Go

Ready: Study your Bible and memorize some verses.

Set: Pray that God will show you where to apply them.

Go: Get out among people, confident and ready to be used.

The In Crowd

Who decides who's popular, anyway?
Do you really want your worth measured
by people who don't always share your values?
God's opinion of you is the only one that counts—
He thinks you're pretty cool.

Try-outs

Ever stand in front of a room full of people trying out for a team
or a part in a play? How scary to have everyone looking at you,
waiting for you to perform! Just smile and do your best.
Jesus is right by your side.

Knowing about God's love isn't enough.
Accepting it, believing it, and being transformed
by it. That is the essence of *experiencing*
God's perfect and matchless love.

CASSIE D. BECK

The Cost

For the price of one soda from the machine every day,
you could really make a difference in some lives.
Have you considered giving to a relief organization?
You're not too young to make an impact.

A Shoulder

What are you known for at school?
When your friends are hurting, do they think
of turning to you for help? Be a comfort—
a shoulder to lean on—so your friends will
open up to you, and then you can share
the love of Jesus with them.

Don't be concerned about the outward beauty of fancy hairstyles, expensive jewelry, or beautiful clothes. You should clothe yourselves instead with the beauty that comes from within, the unfading beauty of a gentle and quiet spirit, which is so precious to God.

1 Peter 3:3–4 NLT

True Blue

It feels so good to be liked! But at what cost?
A true friend never gossips or lets other people talk badly
about her friend. Being popular isn't worth hurting
someone you love.

Ride the Wave

It's hard work for a surfer to paddle out to the humongous waves. Then she has to balance atop her board before she can catch the big wave and ride it back in. The exhilaration of that ride is worth the hard work it took to get there.

Even Nice Words Can Hurt

Ever say something and wish you could suck the words right back? Like ask a someone when her baby's due only to find out she isn't pregnant? Even well-intentioned words can sting. Think before you speak.

Me, a missionary? You can bring God's love to your school.
As you get ready each morning, ask God to show you which
teacher, classmate, janitor, or cafeteria worker needs to hear
a kind word or a simple "God bless you."

SHARON GRIMES

All Shapes and Sizes

Families with Mom, Dad, and 2.5 kids living in the same house with a dog and a cat are rare these days. Embrace the family you have—whatever shape or size it is. God handpicked them just for you.

Girl Talk

Boys think girls are silly with all the whispering and giggling we do.
And boys are kind of gross sometimes, aren't they? It's okay—
it was God's plan that boys and girls would be different.
Have fun with it!

Pen and Paper

E-mails are good. Phone calls are great.
But what about pulling out some paper and
a pen and writing someone a handwritten note?
The special thought and time you took will mean
so much to the person who receives it.

Fruit of the Spirit: Love

When you have the Holy Spirit guiding you, love is evident.
Love is patient with other people. It's kind to everyone.
It forgives easily and doesn't hold grudges. Love is Jesus.

Scraper or Biter?

How do you eat your Oreo?
Do you pull it apart and scrape the filling,
or do you bite the whole cookie? Or maybe
you've found a third way to do it. Is there a right
or wrong way? It's okay to be different!

Consider the Lilies

God dressed the fields with beautiful flowers.
He knows every single bird that falls to the ground.
He has every hair on your head numbered.
Trust Him to take care of you.

Perfume

Ever turn your head at the smell of perfume when someone walks by? Scents are powerful, memorable, and enticing. Your prayers are like perfume to your Father.

The Servant Pyramid

Bosses are at the top of the pyramid and their employees fill the various levels below, right? It's exactly the opposite in the Church. Christ, the head of all, is at the bottom, serving His followers.

They're Watching!

What you say and do will affect what other people think about Jesus. What kind of influence do you want to have?

What a Rush!

Ever ride a roller coaster? Your heart starts beating and your adrenaline builds. It's intoxicating! That excitement is how the angels feel when an unbeliever turns to God. There is no adrenaline rush that even comes close to that one!

In and Out

One day you're in; the next day you're out. Little things—
sometimes nothing—will make friends turn on each
other. Jesus will never leave you or turn His back on you.
That's a promise.

Giving Back

Stop what you're doing and think about what people have done for you. Teachers, leaders, pastors, parents, family members. . . Give yourself a challenge to personally thank someone every day this week.

Whenever I see someone sitting alone—especially someone old—I smile and say something nice. It always makes me feel good to see the person's face light up—I know I've made someone's grandma or grandpa very happy.

Debi Lee

Valentine Hearts

If God had a bowl of those little Valentine candy hearts
for you to snack on, they would read:

Love U!

Died 4 U!

UR Mine!

Fruit of the Spirit: Joy

Another proof of the Holy Spirit is joy. Joy is different than happiness because it comes from inside. It's not dependent on anything that happens—it comes from who you *are*, not what you *experience*.

Missionary Dating

"If he's around me long enough, he'll change." That's an age-old lie of the devil. Don't fall for it. When the time is right for you to date, look for people who share your values and your faith. Those are two of your most important things—why settle for less?

Don't fret or worry. Instead of worrying, pray.
Let petitions and praises shape your worries into prayers,
letting God know your concerns. Before you know it,
a sense of God's wholeness, everything coming together
for good, will come and settle you down.

<small>PHILIPPIANS 4:6 MSG</small>

I Quit

It's easy to throw your hands up in the air and walk away sometimes, isn't it? It's often much harder to tough it out. When you feel like quitting, try one more hour, one more day, one more week. Eventually you'll finish what you started.

I believe in Christianity as I believe that the sun has risen,
not only because I see it, but because by it
I see everything else.

C. S. LEWIS

Embrace Change

Change is hard for everyone. There's always something good
to cling to, though. Moving? Look for something special about
the new place. Going on to a new grade or school? Think of
the new people you'll meet. Dad lose his job? Think of the
possibilities of the new one he'll get.

Lord, make me an ever-radiant shade that shines beautifully for You in every setting!

CASSIE D. BECK

We're all creative in some way. Do you sing, play an instrument, write, act, or draw? Dig deeply into the secret places of your soul and discover the artist within you. Explore, express, and experience God's design for you!

SHARON GRIMES

At a Discount

If you have a little patience, you can find anything at a
discount. And often, if you wait a little while to buy it,
you'll find you don't want it that much anymore anyway.
Patience will keep money in your pocket.

Fruit of the Spirit: Peace

The Holy Spirit wants to bring peace through you. If you're walking side by side with the Holy Spirit, you won't be the one to cause arguments; you'll be the one who brings about peace.

Chores. . .Ugh!

Is it fair that your parents make you do things around the house like the dishes or cleaning your room? You might not enjoy it, but it's fair. Do your part to support the functioning of your family. Even better, do it with a smile.

Pets

Are you a dog lover or a cat person? Or maybe you like birds or fish.
Did you know that God knows every detail about them?
The Bible says that He even cares when a sparrow falls to
the ground. How much more He must care for you,
whom He made in His own image.

Thank-you Note

Up for a challenge? Send a note to three people who have touched your heart in some way—a youth pastor, a favorite aunt, a Sunday school teacher. . . . Let them know their efforts made a difference in your life.

"For I know the plans I have for you," declares the Lord, "plans to prosper you and not to harm you, plans to give you hope and a future. Then you will call upon me and come and pray to me, and I will listen to you. You will seek me and find me when you seek me with all your heart."

JEREMIAH 29:11–13 NIV

Losin' It

Life is hard sometimes. Grief, pain, and sadness are a part of it. Losing a loved one is one of life's most difficult things. When that happens, remember that Jesus is right by your side. Look to Him for comfort.

Guardian Angels

Do you believe they're real? Angels are involved in your life—
protecting you, fighting for you, watching out for you.
When you tuck into bed safely at the end of each day,
thank God for providing that protection.

WWYD?

We talk about what would Jesus do? But what would *you* do? What kind of reputation do you have? What do people assume about you? Live in such a way that people will wonder, *WWYD?*

Roses Are Red

Roses are red
Violets are blue
Jesus loves you
And He died for you, too.

But the Lord said to Samuel, "Don't judge by his appearance or height, for I have rejected him. The Lord doesn't see things the way you see them. People judge by outward appearance, but the Lord looks at the heart."

1 Samuel 16:7 nlt

Side Salad, No Dressing

Oh, puhleeze! Don't worry about your weight.
Just live a healthy life. If you start dieting now,
you'll be doing it forever. Be active and make wise choices,
and your body will become what God intended.

What They Don't Know. . .

. . .will hurt you. It's tempting to try new things and hope Mom and Dad don't find out. Movies. Books. Television shows. Parties. But those boundaries are in place for your own good. Be faithful to their trust.

Accountability

It's about being real with someone. Is there someone you can be completely honest with about your thoughts and sins? A good accountability partner won't judge you but will pray for you and help you with your struggles.

Hang Out with Jesus

If you didn't spend time with your friends, you'd grow apart, right? Having a chat with God and reading from His Word every day is the best way to get to know Him.

Less Is More

Pick one facial feature—eyes, lips, or cheeks—to highlight, and downplay the rest. For example, use eye shadow and mascara on your eyes, but only clear gloss on your lips. Heavy makeup on more than one feature can look clownish rather than pretty.

Clique-clack

A clique is a tight group of friends that doesn't easily open to outsiders. On one hand, the idea of loyalty like that is good. On the other, Jesus doesn't want you to be hurtful by excluding other people.

Driver's Ed. 101

1. Read the Driver's Manual: the Bible!
2. Ask for directions: Get wise counsel!
3. Always keep your eyes on the road: Stay focused; don't get sidetracked!
4. Avoid the use of cell phones while driving: Talk to God instead!
5. Relax, but never fall asleep behind the wheel: Trust God and stay engaged!

CASSIE D. BECK

A Mirror to Your Soul

A mirror reflects your appearance—it's totally honest and shows you exactly what other people see. When you hold the Bible up to your life, it reveals the truth about your life. Make sure your lifestyle reflects Jesus in the mirror of the Bible.

Move Your Body

Your body is a machine—God designed it to move.
Technology makes it possible to sit still while being entertained
the entire day. Instead, ride your bike, go for a jog,
join a sports team. Don't let your machine get rusty.

Two Recipes

"Every girl should know how to whip up two recipes."
It's actually pretty good advice. This would be a good time
for you to learn to make a dinner and a dessert.
That way you're ready to serve and impress.

Diamond in the Rough

Diamonds are mined from deep within the ground. It's amazing that anyone can find them buried under all the dirt and grime. Look around your school. Are there diamonds that need to be pulled from the rough, dusted off, and shined up?

Pretty Please?

God will always give you what you want
if it's in line with His will for you.

Delight yourself in the Lord and he will give you
the desires of your heart.

PSALM 37:4 NIV

Hadassah

Queen Esther—God used her to save the nation of Israel.
She was a young woman with no real power of any kind.
Those kinds of empty vessels are the ones God loves to work
through. Open yourself up to God so He can do great
things through you.

Abilities

People with disabilities often get teased in school for what they *can't* do. How about turning things around by praising them for what they *can* do?

Outside of In

Stand outside the in crowd, and take a look inside.
What do you see? Sometimes it's not very pretty—
backstabbing, pride, arrogance. It's okay to not be the most
popular girl in school if it means being true to yourself.

Walk the Walk

If you talk about godly things at church and then do something opposite at school, you're talking the talk but not walking the walk. Be sure your words and actions line up with God's Word.

Between You and God

Got something on your mind? A big secret? Something burning to spill out? Share it with God. Not only is He the best counselor, but He won't break your trust. Your secret is 100 percent safe with Him.

Femininity

As girls, we can be athletic, sporty, gritty, active, sweaty.
But we can also get pretty and be girly.
Enjoy the frilly stuff sometimes.

Flip-Flop

Do you keep your promises, or do you flip-flop and go
with whatever seems better at the moment? There will always
be something to entice you away from the right thing, but none
of it is worth breaking your word and earning a bad reputation.

How Are You?

That simple question is friendly, concerned, attentive,
and mature. Ask the question then wait for the answer.
Even better still is to ask a follow-up question.

How are you?
Oh? How long have you been feeling ill?
I'm very sorry to hear that. I'll be praying for you.

Face the Music

Mess up? Yeah. We've all been there. The best thing you can do in that situation is to take responsibility for what you did. Fess up, ask forgiveness, and move on.

Take 46

Try, try again. Nothing wrong with not getting it just right the first time. The problem is when you give up and don't keep trying.

Drama Queen

Okay, it's true: Girls can get a little dramatic. Let's face it.
Just don't let drama cause you to overreact or exaggerate.

Step of Faith

Trust in the Lord with all your heart;
do not depend on your own understanding.
Seek his will in all you do, and he will
show you which path to take.

PROVERBS 3:5–6 NLT

Paper Money

Debit cards and credit cards allow us to use less and less paper money. So much so that we're buried under a mountain of debt that will take generations to dig through. Make a choice for yourself: If you can't pay for it, don't buy it.

Gracebook

What's your "Gracebook" status?
Forgiven.

Can You Keep a Secret?

No, seriously. . .can you? People need to be able to trust you—
it's how you'll get into their hearts and be able to make a difference
in their lives. Untrustworthiness is a bad reputation to have.

Miracles All Around You

Take a look out the window. Can you even begin to count the miracles within sight? Think of the world—the universe. For every grain of sand on the beach, there's a miracle that God created around you.

What? Me Worry?

Girls worry; boys don't. That's a big generalization, but girls tend to worry about the future. Boys might be concerned about finding another potato chip in the bag. Not saying one style is better—both have pros and cons—but if you know what the differences are, you can embrace them.

Want More?

There's always more. The key is to learn to be satisfied and grateful. Then, when the "more" comes, you're even more satisfied and grateful. If you always demand the next thing, you'll never really be satisfied.

Keep It Real

No sense trying to be someone you're not.
You're awesome just like you are! God said so!

A Fork in the Road

Decisions are like that. You arrive at a moment
when the road divides and your choice will take you
in one direction or the other. Take the path Jesus
is standing on. You can't go wrong.

An Extreme Makeover

Have you ever seen one of those makeover shows where the woman comes out looking glamorous and basically nothing like she did at the start of the show? Let Jesus give you an extreme inside makeover.

Honor and enjoy your Creator while you're still young,
Before the years take their toll and your vigor wanes,
Before your vision dims and the world blurs
And the winter years keep you close to the fire.

ECCLESIASTES 12:1 MSG

Free Will

How would you feel if someone was your friend because she was forced to be? It wouldn't be very special, would it? It's the same with Jesus. He doesn't want you to follow Him because you have to. He longs for you to want to be with Him.

Eat Your Veggies

Balanced meals. Vegetables. Vitamins. Those are all ways to keep your body healthy. How about your heart? God's Word—the Bible—is healthy food for your soul.

An Undivided Heart

Is your heart divided between two masters? Does God receive a small piece of your devotion while you keep the rest for yourself? Having a divided heart—one that is not fully and solely in the Master's hand—is a very risky way to live.

Fruit of the Spirit: Gentleness

When we hear the word *gentleness* we think of babies
or a gentle breeze. But we need to be gentle with
other people's feelings, tender in the way we correct
and humble in how we approach our success.

Not 10 Percent, 100 Percent

Tithing means giving 10 percent to God via the Church or missions. But really, it's all His. Hold your money with an open hand, ready to do what He calls you to do with it, rather than with a closed fist, clinging to what's not really yours.

Salt and Light

Salt seasons food, preserves meat, sanitizes, cleans, disinfects, and adds flavor. Light shines into darkness. Those two qualities allow Christians to make a difference in the world.

Talent Show

Some girls are musical; some are creative in other ways.
Some do a great job with little children; some prefer caring
for the elderly. No job is better or more important than another.
God designed it so all of the jobs work together perfectly.

Honor Roll

School can be so boring! Still, do your best. The honor roll, or the best grades you're capable of, will build a sense of accomplishment in you. Don't start settling for *good enough* already. It will only lead you to mediocre things.

God Is Love

As hard as you might try, you can't blend oil and water.
In the same way, hate and love are two emotions that
cannot exist together. It is impossible to know God but live
with hate and bitterness toward others.

Best Friends

There's only one thing better than having a praying friend:
being a praying friend.

Be a Lady

Jesus wants your inner beauty to be more important to you than your outward appearance. He doesn't care about your hairstyle, your fancy clothes, or your makeup. He's far more interested in how you treat others. Be kind, generous, calm, compassionate. Be a lady.

The Way the Wind Blows

You can't see wind, but you can see what happens
when it blows. The hand of God is like the blowing wind.
We can't actually see it move, but we can see
what happens when it does.

Costume Jewelry

Costume jewelry costs very little, but often looks just like the real thing. Be sure your heart is decorated with real gems. Don't worry about covering the outside with worthless junk.

Tithe of Time

What if you took inventory of the other assets
in your life—not just money—and tithed on those?
Your other assets include your time, energy, and creativity.

Make Some Waves

Christians are called to take a stand and teach others about their wrongdoings. Yep, even at your age. No one wants to be the outsider, but Jesus was the biggest outsider of all. Show Jesus how much you love Him by being willing to reject wrong and take a stand for right.

Honor Mom and Dad

Are your parents tough on you sometimes?
God's plan is for them to train you now so you'll
remember the important things when you're an adult.
So, honoring your parents as they follow God's plan
is like honoring God Himself.

Lamplight

When the lights are off, it's easy to stumble and stub your toe.
The same is true when you are in the dark spiritually.
God's Word will light your path through life and help
you avoid a painful walk through the dark.

A Ticket to Heaven

There is only one way into heaven—one ticket through Jesus Christ. He has already bought your ticket and has freely offered it to you. You only need to receive it.

"All My Friends Are Doing It!"

It's simply not true—not all of your friends. Truly.
But even if they were, why is that a foundation for an argument?
The fact that all of your friends are doing it
(which they aren't) doesn't make it right.

When No One Is Looking

Who you are is determined by what you do when you think no one is looking. Choices made in secret build a lasting reputation. Even when no one else sees, God sees the good that you do, and He will reward you for it.

Grrrrr

Complainers are no fun! Some people even seem to like being miserable. Focus more on the things that go right. Most of the other stuff isn't worth remembering anyway.

Sequins and Lace

Don't rush the days of flip-flops for high-heeled shoes,
sparkly clothes, and makeup. Everything has its moment
and purpose. You hang in a delicate balance right now.
You're too young to be old, but you feel too old to be
young. So what do you do? You are right where
God wants you to be. . .enjoy it!

For ever since the world was created, people have seen the earth and sky. Through everything God made, they can clearly see his invisible qualities—his eternal power and divine nature. So they have no excuse for not knowing God.

ROMANS 1:20 NLT

"Be Careful, Little Eyes"

Songs like that one you sang as a little girl contain much truth. Even a little bit of the world's poison will take hold and slowly begin to affect your behavior. Ask Jesus to help you keep your mind and thoughts pure and unaffected by the world.

Guard Your Heart

Your heart is your most precious possession.
Reserve it only for God; don't spread around bits
and pieces of it to different boyfriends. He'll let you know
when the time is right to open up to love.

Immediate Obedience

Even when you don't understand His guidance,
your heavenly Father looks out for your best interests.
Learn to immediately obey His voice without question.

Stand Your Ground

Imagine that you're standing on a chair with your best friend standing on the ground right in front of you. Take her hand, and pull her up onto the chair. That would be hard, wouldn't it? Now imagine that she pulls you down from the chair. Pretty easy, huh? It's far easier to pull someone down than it is to pull someone up.

Take One for the Team

You can't always get what you want. Sometimes it's necessary to make a sacrifice for the greater good of others. It's good to put your own wants and needs behind what other people want in order to show the love of Christ.

No Surprises

God knew what He was doing when He created you. . .
just the way He wanted you.

*"I knew you before I formed you in your mother's womb.
Before you were born I set you apart."*

JEREMIAH 1:5 NLT

Skeptics and Cynics

You can see the love of Jesus in the eyes of a newborn baby. You can see the paintbrush of God in the colors of a sunset. It's impossible, when looking at His creation, to even consider that He doesn't exist.

The Company You Keep

Jesus wants us to be part of the world around us so we can make an impact. That can only be accomplished when we purpose to only be "joined" or united with people who share our love for Jesus and our goal of pleasing Him with our lifestyle. The company you keep will tell others who you are.

"My Parents Drive Me Crazy!"

Boring rules! It would be awesome to have the freedom
your friends have, wouldn't it? The thing is, if your parents
lightened up and allowed you to do more, it would be going
against God's will for them. You don't want that, do you?

Don't Go There

If you are in doubt about what is right or wrong,
just ask yourself how you would feel if someone did it to you.
If you hesitate, even briefly, then don't go there.

Church Is Not Just a Building

A church service might happen in a building structure, but *the Church* is far more than four walls and a roof. *The Church* is the body of Christ. While you can worship God anywhere, God created us to fellowship with other Christians. Be faithful in meeting with God's people each week.

Who Am I?

If you had to describe yourself, what would you say?
Would you talk about outward appearance or the things you have?
"I'm blond and live with my parents. . . ." Instead, dig deeper.
Learn your true identity—the way God sees you.

Fruit of the Spirit: Self-control

If a little's good, a lot must be better, right? Not always.
It's important to exercise self-control over even the little
things in life. Moderation in everything will create
balance in your life.

Glass Half-Full

Only listen to people who want what's right for your life.
Avoid cynical and sarcastic friends who want to see you turn
from good and run toward evil. Your thoughts will run your life;
make sure you feed your mind the things of God.

Reality Television

Did you know most of those shows are scripted in some way? Scripted reality? Doesn't make sense, does it? Truth is, the only reality is your own. Don't hold yourself to some Hollywood standard for appearance, dress, success, body image, financial status, etc. None of it's even real.

It's All about Choices!

Everything you do in life—big or small—
comes back to a choice you made. It's important to
decide ahead of time what you'll do when the pressure
hits so you're prepared with your response. Then stick
to your choice even when it's difficult.

*And whatever you do, whether in word or deed,
do it all in the name of the Lord Jesus, giving thanks
to God the Father through him.*

COLOSSIANS 3:17 NIV

Flirting Is Fraud

Coyly giggling. Teasing. Making suggestive comments.
Flirting is nothing more than false advertising.
Even worse, it's tempting boys into the sin of lust.
It's not cute at all. Be friendly, but not flirtatious.

Fabric Softener

You know those dryer sheets that go in with the wet clothes?
They tumble around together in the heat and the clothes come
out softer and they smell great. The Bible is like fabric softener.
Don't forget to toss it in every day so it can tumble around
with you as the world heats up.

Hidden in Your Heart

How are you on scripture memorization?
It's an important part of preparing for battle in this world.
When you hide God's Word in your heart, He'll bring it
to your memory when the tough times hit.

It's a Barbie World

Based on her measurements, if Barbie were a real person she'd be about six feet tall and would only weigh around 100 pounds. Her proportions are physically impossible. Don't hold yourself to an unrealistic standard like that.

Concealer

Ever had a pimple? Those annoying and ugly red spots
right on your nose or in the center of your cheek?
Sometimes we have blemishes on our soul or on our
reputations. Let the Holy Spirit conceal them with
God's grace through forgiveness.

Frog in Water

If you drop a frog into a pot of boiling water, he'll jump right out. But if you put the frog in cold water and then turn up the heat, he'll adapt to the changing temperature and stay put until he boils to death. Your school is like that pot of cold water. Make sure you don't sit still until the water boils.

Nothing to Lose

Get nervous about sharing your faith? Just go for it!
You've got nothing to lose and everything to gain.
Your friends need you to point them to the cross.
If you don't, who will?

To-do List

1. Pick someone first who is usually chosen last.
2. Compliment the girl who doesn't often hear nice things about herself.
3. Sit next to the one who always sits alone on the bus.
4. Thank a teacher for helping you learn.
5. Tell your mom how glad you are to have her.
6. Call your grandma to chat.

DEBI LEE

Just the Leftovers?

After your day is divided up between school, fun, friends, parents, sports, clubs, and church activities, what's left for God? Make your time with God the most important part, and then give everything else the leftovers.

Allowance

When you have money, how do you decide what to do with it?
God asks that you give 10 percent back to Him as a symbol of
your gratitude and faith. Yep, that even means you. There's no age
requirement for giving. In fact, if you start now and make it
a habit, it'll be much easier to stick to it for your whole life.

Ad Campaign

Designers work really hard to make the perfect,
most appealing ad so their product will sell.
You're like a walking billboard for Jesus. Are you
living in a way that leads people to Him?

Why Does Everything Change?

It feels like nothing ever stays the same, right? Well, it's true.
Your whole life is about change—that's one thing that
won't change. Embrace it, and look for the new things
God wants you to learn and enjoy.

ABC, 123

There are simple truths in scripture:

A: Jesus loves you.

B: He died for you.

C: He forgives your sins. . .

1:   . . .all you have to do is ask Him.

2:   Live for Him.

3:   Share His love with others.

And don't let anyone put you down because you're young.
Teach believers with your life: by word, by demeanor,
by love, by faith, by integrity. Stay at your post reading Scripture,
giving counsel, teaching.

1 Timothy 4:12 msg

Fact vs. Opinion

What's your favorite song? That's an opinion question.
Most people will have a different answer and that's okay.
Is Jesus the Son of God who came to earth to die
for us and take away our sins? That's a fact question.
There's only *one* answer.

Fruit of the Spirit: Patience

It's so hard to wait for things. God's timing is best, though. If you ask for His guidance, the Holy Spirit in you will help you know God's timing and then teach you the patience to wait for it.

When peers push you to fit in, trust your inner voice.
If you feel uncomfortable wearing or doing something,
don't do it. Your friends will think you're strong
and independent.

CHERYL EKLUND

False Fronts

The world is full of *fake*. False eyelashes, fixed body parts—
even makeup is like a touched-up image of who you really are.
Be comfortable with yourself and love the *you* God made you
to be without worrying about being someone you're not.

Say Cheese!

That warning is just enough time to pose for the camera that's about to snap. As a Christian, you need to be "camera ready" at all times. The world is watching, just waiting for you mess to up. Be ready to smile for Jesus.

Never Give Up

Changing your mind and moving on to something else is different
than giving up and quitting. Make sure you think hard before
giving in to failure. Often, just before everything clicks,
it seems the worst. Don't miss out on the reward of the *click*.

There's No Place Like Home

Dorothy had it right. There really is no place like home.
But most of us don't have ruby slippers we can click
to be transported safely back to our bedrooms.
Be careful about the situations you find yourself in—
it's not always easy to get out of them.

Apples to Apples

You can't compare an apple to an orange. They each have a unique look, taste, and feel. They even offer different health benefits. The same is true for you and your classmates. You're all completely different physically, intellectually, and emotionally. There's no point in comparing. Just do your very best.

Three-way Mirror

Ever pulled a shirt a little lower? Pulled up a skirt a tad shorter? Bought a size tighter? Looked at the rear view of a pair of jeans you were trying on? If you're trying to entice the boys, you're putting them at risk for lust, which is the same as adultery. (See Matthew 5:28)

It's so easy to ask God for help when in need, but don't forget to thank God for the good things. It's amazing to stop and reflect on God's goodness in the middle of the chaos of life.

CHERYL EKLUND

Decisions, Decisions

How do you know which way to go? Simple:
Pray for God's guidance and look in His Word.
He'll make it clear to you. If you're still not sure,
do nothing until He points the way.

Aber-Holli-Crombie. . .Who?

Name brands are so important to girls. . .but why?
What's the point? By the time you're buying your own
clothes, the ones you love now won't even be popular,
and you'll want to spend less on your stuff anyway.
Why not start making more responsible choices now?

But grow in the grace and knowledge of our Lord and Savior Jesus Christ. To him be glory both now and forever! Amen.

2 PETER 3:18 NIV

In Between

Ever feel like you're dangling between two worlds: church and school? They're so different, yet you feel at home in either place. How's that possible? It's because Jesus goes *with* you rather than waiting for you to come to Him.

In my teens, I was approached by a total stranger who said, "You're Kae Cameron's daughter. I'd recognize her face anywhere!" How I long for the day when people look at my life and say, "Oh, you must be a daughter of the heavenly Father. I'd recognize His face anywhere!"

KATHERINE WALDEN

Prodigal

The prodigal son was a young man who left his father's home and chose a life of sin. He wandered far away and had a hard time getting back home. When he did, though, his father welcomed him with open arms. Have you wandered from your heavenly Father? He's waiting with open arms.

Do-gooder, or Good-doer?

The result looks the same—good deeds.
But a do-gooder wants to look good and get praised
for the deeds. A good-doer only desires to do right
and please God. Be a good-doer.

Green-eyed Monster

Jealousy is distasteful to God and to others. Be happy for your friends when they get something or achieve something they've worked hard for. Even better—want it more for them than you want it for yourself.

Boys Are Messy. . .

. . .and, let's face it, sometimes a little smelly, right?
God made us all different, and the things you find
gross about boys now will one day be a reason
that you like them.

What is your favorite way to experience God's creation?
Take time to look at the clouds, trees, plants, and flowers.
Each one has its own individual beauty, just like you do.
Celebrate your unique style, personality, and beauty.

Sharon Grimes

Thankfulness

Think of ten ways God has blessed you.
Tell Him out loud that you're thankful for
the many ways He's made your life rich.

Musical Chairs

The music stops playing and eleven participants scramble
for ten chairs. Someone always has to lose—it's part of the game.
Losing isn't the problem, not playing is. Play the game of life;
sometimes you win, sometimes you don't. Just stay in the game.

The Purpose of Dating Is Not. . .

to eat at good restaurants and see the latest movies.
to spend time with the cutest boys.
to make your friends jealous.
to feel good about yourself.

The Purpose of Dating Is. . .

to find the mate God has chosen for you.

If you're not ready for that,
you're not ready to date.

Pretty as a Picture

Grandmas say that all the time. It's weird because pictures aren't always pretty. But you know what? To grandmas they are. Same with God. Where the world might see plain, He sees radiant beauty.

Charm is deceptive, and beauty does not last;
but a woman who fears the Lord will be greatly praised.

PROVERBS 31:30 NLT

Text Me

Everywhere you look, girls have their phones open to a
keyboard and their fingers are working furiously to
communicate with someone. Try pray-texting God just for fun.
Type out the text and send it to yourself.

When Good Girls Do Nothing

It's great to avoid bad behavior. It's even better to do something about it. Be a good influence; stand up for truth. Defend weaker people. Do something.

A No-reason Call

Want to make someone's day? Call her for no reason.
Grandma, youth leader, pastor's wife, etc. Just dial the phone and
let her know you appreciate her. Nothing else. People are used to
getting calls when someone wants something. How awesome to
get a call just because.

Charm Bracelet

Charms dangle delicately from the links of a bracelet—
often a symbol of a place, time, or achievement of some
kind. What charm would you choose to represent this
week? A sport? TV? Praying hands? An open Bible?
How you spend your time decides the charm.

Glass Slippers

Cinderella's glass slippers were an indentifying marker to prove who she was. Everyone in the land was measured against those glass slippers, but they all proved to be imposters.

What identifies you as a daughter of the King?

A Moment of Praise

Most people know what prayer is. Thankfulness is easy, too. But praise requires you to step out of your comfort zone and give glory to a mighty God. How do you praise Him? Words? Song? Actions? Be sure to praise God every day.

The measure of success is not whether you have tough problems to deal with, but whether it is the same problem you had last year.

JOHN FOSTER DULLES

Sticks and stones may break my bones, but words will never hurt me. False. Most bullying is done by words, and words do hurt. Take action. Stand up to bullies, protect the innocent, and make friends with the weak. You can change someone's life.

CHERYL EKLUND

"I'll Pray for You"

Most of us say those words. But do we follow through?
Have you ever said, "I wish I could help. But I'll at least pray."
At least? Praying for someone is the most loving and uplifting thing
you can do. Offer that first, not last. Then keep your promise.

Time Flies When You're Having Fun

Fifth grade. Sixth grade, seventh, eighth. . .
It goes so fast. Be sure to make each year special
by leaving a mark of God's grace as you pass through.

Circle Yes or No

While you need to be nice to everyone, you don't have to be everyone's best friend. It's good to limit those people you let close to your heart. Choose your friendships wisely and protect yourself by guarding your privacy.

Your Brain: An iPod

iPods are pretty cool. You can load them up with your favorite music. You can even subscribe to radio shows, podcasts, and all sorts of cool things by syncing them up to your computer. Sync your brain to God by plugging into His iTunes, the Bible.

Sugar and Spice

That's what girls are made of. Ever heard that rhyme?
It means that girls are sweet and gentle, but also sassy.
It's a good thing to be multidimensional, but it's not good if
you can't control your emotions or actions. Pray for self-control.

If you love learning, you love the discipline that goes with it—how shortsighted to refuse correction!

PROVERBS 12:1 MSG

A Roller Coaster

Peaks, valleys, hairpin turns, steep drops, loops. . .roller coasters
are so fun! Life's the same way. What if you saw it as a ride and
went with it, whatever came around the next bend? You'd be able
to relax and enjoy the ride without worrying.

Relax

You didn't start the work in you, and you don't have to finish it on your own. He's got it covered.

God in Twitter Speak

I love U, My child. I died 4 U. Accept My grace, then lean on Me.
It's the easy way. Tell ur friends I love them, too.

True Friends

You have to be a friend to have a friend. You know the command to do to others like you want them to do to you? That's the best recipe for friendship.

But, Mom!

To be honest, as hard as it is, you shouldn't say that.
Think about it: Those words, spoken like that, are argumentative,
whiny, and make you seem immature. The best idea is to obey
first then go back later to discuss why you might want to do
things differently next time.

Work-for-hire

Need some cash? There's plenty you can do:
babysit, extra chores, shovel snow or rake leaves
for a neighbor. Plan ahead for saving and giving,
and then make wise choices with the rest.

*Look in the mirror and find one thing that is unique
to only you. Thank God for making you special.*

CHERYL EKLUND

Take a Chance

Whatever it is: Trying out for a team, singing a solo, doing the school play. . .go for it! Why not? Pray that God would strengthen you and stand strong beside you, holding you up. Nervousness is good—it means growth.

Clothed in Christ

That's one of those phrases they say in church, but unless you stop and think about it, it doesn't make much sense, does it? Imagine it's like putting Jesus on as your clothing every day so others see Him when they look at you. What a cool concept!

Fruit of the Spirit: Kindness

A scared girl with Down's syndrome reached a hand out for the captain of the football team. He kindly took her hand and led her to her class. That's kindness. That's Jesus.

Are You a Jesus Freak?

Anyone ever call you that? It might sound like an insult—maybe that person even meant it as an insult. But really, it's the nicest thing anyone could call you. Grin and be thankful that someone saw Jesus in you.